ON THE INSIDE

ON THE INSIDE

Clive Matson

Graphics by David Kelso

CHERRY VALLEY EDITIONS

The poet wishes to thank the many people who gave him feedback and encouragement in writing this poem, among them Nina Mayer, John Ceely, Jana Harris, Chuck Cohen, Sharon Stout and Terry Hill.

Copyright © 1982 by Clive Matson. All rights reserved.
First edition.
Graphics reproduced by permission of the artist.

Publication of this book was made possible in part by a grant from the National Endowment for the Arts, a federal agency, in Washington, D.C.

Library of Congress Cataloging in Publication Data:

Matson, Clive, 1941–
   On the inside.

   I. Title.
PS3563.A83705   1982   811'.54   82-14621
ISBN 0-916156-65-6

Design by the poet, David Kelso, Naomi Schiff and Nina Mayer. Photo by Naomi Schiff. Graphics technology by Oscar Serley. Typography by Susan Young and Ann Flanagan Typography.

CHERRY VALLEY EDITIONS are distributed by
Writers & Books, 892 South Clinton Avenue,
Rochester, NY 14620

This poem is for people to use.

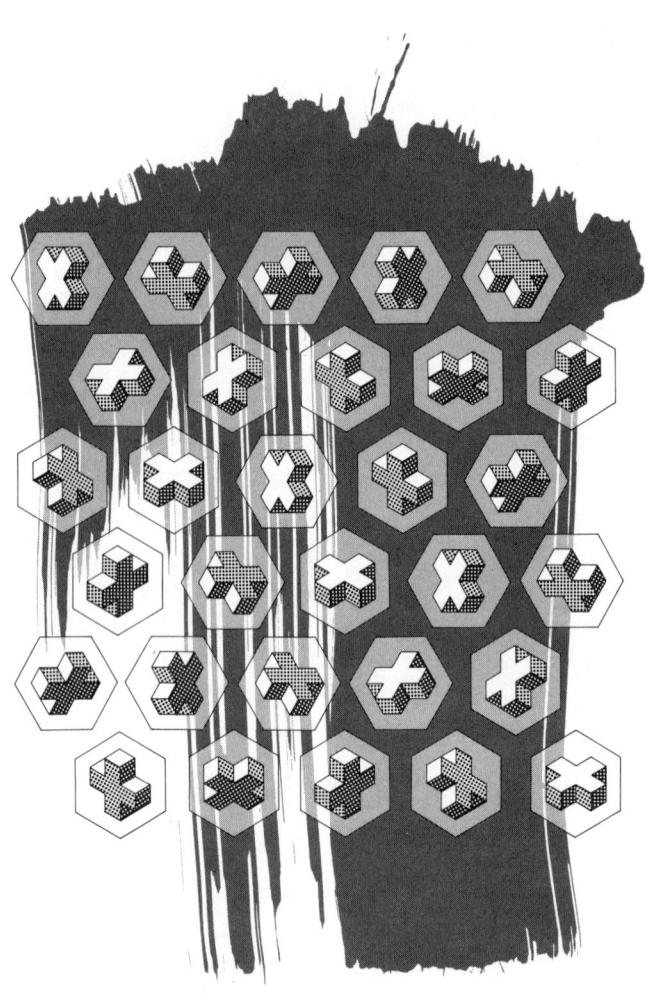

One

Here: gentle anarchy describes
the daily lives we call our own.

Friends' faces are smiling or cool,

Chuck purses lips as he puzzles out a pattern,
Mal faces straight-on relaxed
with muscled hands at sides,
with hair flaming and eyes sizzling
Peter stops, displays an all-present mind.

Linda stranded on a beach scans her credit,
phones collect and is accepted,
Rachel measures well-known pain
against what she knows is right
and tilts her head to the side,
Evelyn lifts her chin getting
what she wants with black pride.

No one rules what we do,
we work out o.k. action between us
with advice from our hearts.

Lines are not down,

sympathetic sound twists out of airwaves
and resounds through black boxes,

plastic discs reverberate
with exact statements of feeling
and overtones of love in a thousand forms,
over the telephone sounds a voice
constructed from someone I'd like to see.

Lines are not down,

another mind is within reach
of metal change dropped in a transit box,

within reach of two legs walking
or an outstretched thumb plus a wait and conversation,
within limits of braced-together machinations
of a gas- and air-burning car.

We are free to gather from near and far,
in work or leisure compare the complicated scenes
that move by on all sides,

we're free to sketch in backgrounds
we're moving along with,
match and explain the sets of our shoulders today
and point out tools and tricks
we've picked up on our way since birth.

Now as before,
like our ancestors, like our parents
we're free to choose partners and friends
from humans within reach,

free to try making our dreams real
from what we're given to dream,
free to map our lives through what's ahead,
to cruise along main routes,
take on challenge of zigzag byways
or balance through untraced wilderness.

Knocked off our feet by unseen consequence
we can feel out support
and squirm over to solid ground,
pick ourselves up and risk standing
in changing light, in an overcast dawn
we're again free to posit future action,

to choose from alleys and roads before us
or to clear an untrod path.

We're free
for the old ways of an old culture
plus a few new variations,
if we're quiet beyond careful boundaries.

Safe with minimum cool

we're free to gather in groups
and raise consciousness to roofs of our skulls,
free to speak unspoken thoughts and share
feelings we were too shy to voice,
free to open mouths and reveal treasures
we've hidden under our tongues

and kept safe from hustling ears and hostile eyes,
safe from the street's blaze.

We're free to develop bodies into smooth flowering,
to train and nurture minds into rounded clarity
behind draped windows,
away from the open street
where the beast rages.

Where the beast rampages,

displays his many veils and casual faces
that masquerade as real beings,
on the inside of this strange prison
his real self is twice hidden:

once behind a mask
and once behind a cocked-back threat
he will carry out,
he will enact upon our backs.

Two

He doesn't carp: he carves lives

into useful shapes, he programs minds
to manipulate his thoughts,
he molds flesh into cogs
for his machine, he bends knees
to scrape clean his shit from the floor,

he rejects whole people like garbage
or trains for violence in ghetto streets

and his schools also teach mistrust of humans,
divide and make tensely productive the people
who are his energy and source of food.

Under pain of poverty, deprivation, disease
he twists humans into multi-faced tools
over all the land where he holds dominion.

The beast dominates: but not here.

Here we live at peace between his paws.

Between walls we make safe,
before jaws clamp shut open view to blue sky
we lay on paint and decoration as magical barricades,
mark table, chair and bed with the shapes
of our bodies as our places,
the enclosed air as our space.

In need of food,
even pushed out from inner sanctuaries
we're given enough room
to escape total domination:

playing mouse to his cat claws,
finding niches around his joints
or not obviously outside his laws
we find enough space
to make money in the strange ways that we can,

feign complicity, learn a trade or craft we enjoy
and mount his ladders dangled with many lures,

in need put on masks in a prostitute dance
to suck bread off the system,
stretch lips to polite smiles
and push anger to the accurate inside.

In bodily need
we rent our skills by the hour,

hire ourselves as slaves for a day
or contract to slice a year into thin sections
of work, errands, sleep and some pleasure,

in bodily need
we can buy and sell on the side.

Molly does people's carpentry,
Truce sells poetry on the street,
A. runs dope one step ahead of paranoia,
Rosemary plays violin in doorways,
Fred and George bang knuckles
on car innards in borrowed driveways,
Solange, Sally, Susan sew by hand,
Jeff, Maggie, Doris, Bill take care of
breadwinners and split their earnings.

The student plays it in
from family, school, government,
the ex-G.I. on the Pentagon's dole,
many-names squeezes loot out of welfare
coming and going, the empty-handed
ask spare change all over the country.

Susan sells hamburgers, Cathy sells land,
Fartel works computers, Bruce ghost-writes books,
Todd sandwiches the year
between shipping out and unemployment,
Laurie, Jane, Bob, Ailie
carefully keep what they've got now,

Lisa, Roger, Marie, Ross go from job to job,
Peggy is well-paid and pushes social change
through the beast's gut anyway.

TAXI splits the gross of a slim business equally,
the Commune puts hands into many crafts,
families feel the pinch twice,
three, four, five times over,

the many peel skin and pare off flesh
to fit under low budgets and still have room,

what room can be found beneath economic barriers
that squeeze down like horizon-wide clamps,
money the name of the heartless game
that vamps on us.

At job interviews, in welfare, when the taxman comes
put off the hungry animal.

Throw the beast his morsel to keep him quiet,
not letting on how much is cupped
under the palm of our hand,
dig deeper in our pockets
or turn up a fool's face if he asks for more.

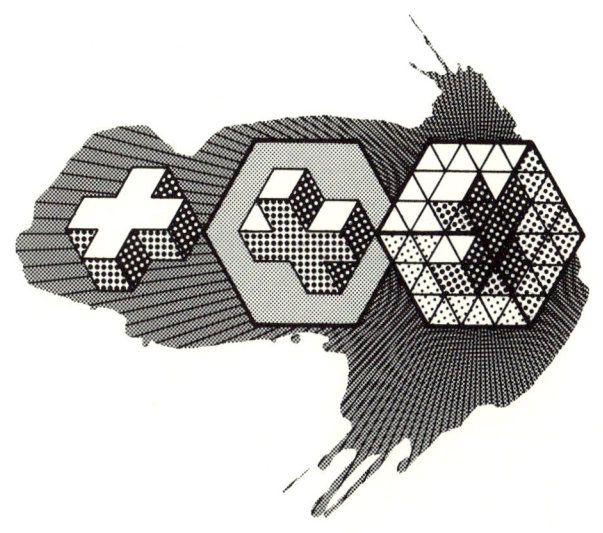

Three

Needing each bit of strength
as apartments and houses squeeze smaller
between rising rents and the dollar's lessening power,

between more people and less popular space
as walls close in
we still possess enough room
to learn how to live together,

assess hearts and arrange new heads,
create or revive attitudes that aid living
under these lowering skies.

Day to day
there's even enough mental space

leisurely to become adept at finding
personal happiness as we follow
the ideal of liberty:
life allows room to do what one wants
so long as others aren't hurt.

Liberty bannered in green and yellow silk,
liberty leading a stream of people
its smooth-cheeked, haloed face so beautiful
the image can cloud our minds

and even wiping celluloid aside
we must struggle, struggle
through dirt and grit of daily grinds
to keep heads so clear
we will be aware when humans are hurt
and blood does flow.

And blood flows.

Metaphoric blood flows freely,
with face bounded by tender bones
humanity bleeds,
drips blood
from mouths' corners, clogging red dribbles
out bashed-up noses and heads
twisted from a hundred ugly collisions.

From a hundred dream perversions
that hook believing humans and spin us far out
on ungrounded courses:

Tracy thought money is the key to happiness
and when his feeling heart caught in his throat
he had no words to carry a breath,
ended in a backwoods trailer, choked,

Marie thought marriage would save her, gave her soul
to her symbol of a fine one:
wine drink and feet up on the couch,
when the wine went sour she axed her mate,

the G.I. believed he'd be a hero in Vietnam
and return to a good job but he came back
in a wheelchair, brought several buddies
home in bags, several others with
no tongues and most everything unsaid,

Cecil and Jay are knocking on doors of the upper class
following slick photos in their minds
and they scramble up stairs unaware
their shoes are stomping on people's heads,

Honey, Moss, Rudy, Brail take off
on drugs, filled with lofty dreams they
soar on balloons and when the air
gets too rarified to breathe they crash,
pull each other down in tangled heaps,

John complains it's the pinching of blood's flow
that oppresses, and Marty's pinched hopelessness
drove him to a sideswiping wreck
and highway patrol pictures,
other's blood on the fenders

and as humans squeeze skulls tighter
I dream we squeeze our entrails out behind.

Have you seen people's minds clamped down,
have you seen eyes with hope shot out,
targets for dreams they couldn't realize?

Kay's sister would correct pain
by putting the best ideas above human suffering,
lays out a most correct line like a
steel wire she tightens over her audience,
straightens meandering loops and cuts through flesh:

blood flows.

Blood flows,
eyes are blanked and gutters filled
with maimed, tortured, and the innocent
about to collide in mind-caging wrecks.

As if coming back from the dead,
stepping out of a street running blood

liberty reasserts its power through sober lips,

"Life allows room to do what one wants"
the clause "so long as others aren't hurt"
binds our acts with double force.

We wipe red splatters off sleeves
the others are so close
and our own safety is an equal bottom line,
we are others' others
and a single flowing vein does sustain
all beings under a common sky.

We've no choice.

On a shrinking world
all loose ends join
and there's no break in the chain of consequence,
others' blood is as significant as my blood,
any rip-off returns blade-up to me
with knife or pen, with sucker or sucker's price
any blood taken is taken from life,
from my life, from all our lives

and shrugging shoulders, uninvolved gestures
accept stamping a death's head
over the planet, skull and crossbones.

No choice.

The lid is on,
pressure is building

and there's no indifferent way to be:
all pleasant variations are flattening
to plus and minus.

The whole game is contained in one move.
And in the next. And in each move after,
and each next move adds to or subtracts from
the one tide that will determine
whether we the species live or die.
Life at mercy of a beacon star
that blinks light or dark. Blinks death
or life with every breath.

We return to care.

To care for life.

Revive care first on physical levels
to level economic changes with bread shared,
door unlocked and refrigerator open
to a circle of family and intimates,
help friends pull themselves
out of gutters and onto the sidewalks
til base ground is up high enough
we can operate as undesperate beings.

Flora, Jim know they're comfortable
and give dinners, the odd job, rent checks,
M. drops a power trip that sucked energy
from lovers and now loves in return,

N. develops a trade and loses the whiny voice
that needed damping, C. does the same.

Donna, Jay, Katherine pool resources and find room
for their cousins, the grandmother, Jay's other son,
Sandy, Ken, Alan, Eva work in crisis centers,
Van gives his talents to a commune, joins healing
with carpenters, gardeners and childrearers,
Jeeter, Leslie give rooms to the needy,
Deward heats up a hot tub,
K., A. open their houses.

Not desperate
we can search for outlines of decency
in ourselves and others, discover a decent human

who can do the fitting thing
as a being alive with other beings,
look to fill half-dreamt postures
with clear, rounded flesh, kind eyes
and spread, firm stance on the ground.

Not desperate
we can give ourselves room
to work out tenets of a new morality,

where a human doesn't use another human,
not as object, not for profit, not for fun,
but works and rests and plays
easy with this term on earth.

I've seen legs lengthen underneath me,
a range of feeling expand inside
and I know there's nothing more beautiful
than a human with faculties alive,

I love the intelligent spark that flies
between eyes of siblings who feel the same
and I despise the scaly hands that prey
on us and make us dangerous.

The streets are uncertain.

Not trained to limit freedom with care,
innocent, undecided or with warring minds
are beings under acrylic and vinyl skins,
behind made-up faces and glad teeth

needy, hungry selves crowd streets
like a carnival going mad.

Four

The beast is inside us. Inside me.

Peel skin off muscle and bone,
turn flesh layers back
and I discover he's half-grown inside
shooting nerves toward my soul,

in my skull long twists
of his gray matter sprout from pictures
he plants in my mind and repeats
in the world outside.

I see his eye in a flickering jewel,
his flesh in a breast almost bared
and muscled ass swing, his breath
in smoke exhaled from a common joint.

Levy complains, complains "being stoned
as a way of life is crippling as TV,"
and dope's power for joyous awareness
pulls dozens, masses into smoke
in the morning, confusion in the evening,

Ned and Cathy wheel in paisley orgy rooms
and spend their energy maintaining balance,
D. delights in Jesus, crowns her head with thorns
and every word she tongues is a barb for God,
Gloria drowns in a spoon, Jim dives in a bottle.

First-sight escapes from pain
only change reflections on inside surfaces
of the beast's transparent cage
where we are trapped,

where we are mapped
and wired for weaknesses,
where images blink around in clusters to distract.

War, sports, styles, soap operas, space flight,
politics are great spectacles performed to distract,
our glossy egos and their idols,
fem beautiful and macho flash
he spotlights on movie screens to distract
us from what's underneath,
from what he snuck in
when we were too young to
scope his wiles and too small
to fend him off:

his blueprint for being.

From parents, from media, from siblings and friends
his phrases drift in, attach
to my mind, rephrase my feelings
and whisper at my inner ear.

Oh throw the beast out. Out.

Sort words apart,
this parasite's from our own,
out the voice that speaks
in super-resonant tones.

We need separation columns for the mind,
a new science to define
which thoughts are his,
to separate the malignant from indifferent
from our own healthy.

Karen gathers words, compares their geometries
against triangles that bound her life
and finds ninety percent incongruent,
Mona, Jerry, Alex talk and talk until late
and how much can they use in life,
whose sense of truth is so fine?

Lecturers, singers, comedians, well-loved gurus
so often seduced by their own followings,
sucked into the star system become
luminaries too high above what's happening
here day to day to see,

    no easy guides! No easy guides
but masks and false voices on all sides.

A pebbly rasp insists that
to listen inward is sick:
we should only act, and beast digits
frame Tokay who listened so hard
his ears sported, now when his name
is called he cannot hear.

A doctor judges Burg insane
so he swallows pills without a murmur,
Davis sank in a quagmire of despair
as she watched one feeling: years lost
stuck in the same clay, Paddy follows orders:
buy and make money, make money and buy,
B. was too good to change: deceased.

Blot the beast out. Out.
Stifle his sly voice
that proclaims there's nothing to decode,
out the feeling I'm too perfect
to change or too weak
to survive some different way.

My head is my property and my proper task
is to know what's in it, to own what's mine
and to ask identity of foreign thoughts,
to assess which to defy and which to accept.

It's our DNA that contains information for life,
our bodies and minds the strength
to stand open-eyed, with nostrils cleared
the strength to follow our noses
and smelling a rat's nest
to sniff out the biggest stink.

And the rankest stench
comes from my own back,
from festering scabs and sores
on backs of those nearby!
How often have I felt limbs claw,
elbows shove others down and aside
as people scramble for positions on high,
who will soon all be equal in ashes?

Dean sharpens claws, his hawk's eye
gleams for human prey as he calculates

when to dive into a stoop,
Margie makes music with her curves' harmonies
and crescendos out her sisters' songs,
Nadine uses proper words to keep her elite pass valid,
Alvin turns on warmth if you've something to give.

The Iceman dies and lives by the score of the game,
X. clambered to get rich,
Y. screwed her partner for gain,
Z. had in mind a honey voice,
Son listened to a dog.

With hopes on a distant haven
the crouched fighter perfects a modern stance
—and whose soldier is this, whose human?

Head a steel-sprung computer spinning through tapes
and flashing targets on inner gunsights,
legs angled in status of a tripod
and torso fuel source for lasers
that fire through whirlpool eyes.

Throw out over-competition. Out.

Not my definition of life, that it's dog eat dog,
"Screw them before they screw you,"
not my definition of humans,
that it's our nature to spew energy
in the clash of figurative swords:
the beast's.

The beast defines us
away from our bodies, bends our minds
into loops and lamellar forms
that deny the whole body exists.

How can we be his dupes,
how be indecent if our bodies are the known,
shared common denominator of life on earth!

How glory in another's death
if we're able fully to imagine our own!

No whiff of niter or gangrene
reached B-52 cabins over Vietnam,
no formaldehyde corrodes noses of stockbrokers
dealing junkfood and healthcare in one portfolio,
nuclear companies' dividend checks
probably don't contain much plutonium.
Muggers' necks don't bleed at knife point,
rapers' lips don't part with screams,
when Oreo had Jerry wrapped around her finger
all she felt was the string.

This woman with petroleum-derived make-up,
artificial hair and no sweat,
would she be object to a male fantasy,
and what's her choice?

This man with legs and shoulders
shaped to a triangle and no felt hormones,

is he a 20th century machine,
his head wired with whose voice?

Whose man is this? Whose woman?

Are we deluded
in a wish to escape our bodies
and push ourselves into alien shapes,
pick up the beast's easy formulas
strewn glittering on foot-trodden streets?

Throw him out. Out.

Useless his flat images of jigsaw people,
painful to my body his narrow molds.

His half selves find other halves in mates,
his proud chauvinists trade minds for hearts
or barter soft skin for strong arms:

Mike, Penny master power by mastering partners,
climb on their backs like on horses
and guide all motion with the knees,
jabbing, loosening, squeezing,
Zim doles out affection in exchange for control,
Sandy Mae gives sex for money and attention:
how commonly do we dangle willing puppets
on threads of feeling! I should know,
having done it so recently
and stayed aloof behind measuring eyes.

On the street Elaine is treated as a hooker,
trained as hooker and maid for the house,
Ben a hitman or eunuch on the streets,
brought up as provider and king of the house.

Oh throw the beast out. Out.

More meaningful partnerships abound
or await our creating,
bountiful too are more kind models
for who we are.

Susan runs a machine, twists knobs and fits wrenches
with fingers whose whorls are human,
Donnie deals with feelings,
laughs, cries and lays back on a spine
as flexible as yours or mine.

Knowing the sternum's sensation
and needing ease in living with it
M. takes to a cave,
slips learned selves off like snakeskins,
N. lets the sun shine on new babe's skin,
steps into the day

where the beast would split us
into sneering beings baring fangs across wastelands,
his bottom line:
if he can't tame us, or confuse us, then divide us
he continues to conquer.

Vultures squawk in crags, demons whisper
at our ears and how many listen, how many flinch
behind a bleached and wasp-like mask?

J. camps behind a limp wrist, flagrantly gay,
Olive bugs eyes with hate, outrageously red-neck,
K. shuts lips on a new tongue, ducks in a closet.

Who can fully conceal the feelings
contained within inches of our skin,
who could camouflage the child
running scared behind hostile eyes?

I do not hide. I come out human, whole,

not so different in what's different
between my legs as the same,
with organs, head, four limbs, torso
and living sternum all shared.

Shared too the wish for a pleasant life,
shared the desire
that faces I meet have eyes not splintered
by the beast's tooth, shared the wish
that we meet and create a net of actual friendship
I hold and am held in and give
back easily my own warm strength.

All shared!
Shared too our weaknesses,

shared the cacophony of voices
within our heads, shared my fear
that a phrase may disarm me
and the beast's claw pushing at my chest
will twist me into a dumb actor
in the beast's robot paradise.

Throw him out. Out.

Five

The world of the mind's images
is mirrored in the world of friends:

postures in living rooms, stances on the street,
expressions, choices of hustles and careers
display such a spectrum of ways to be
I need clear sight and explicit information
to sort whose tool who might be,
and how, where the beast
has been, is now and what angle
he'll slant in on next.

His images, his twisted paradigms
wing through midnight barricades like bats
with apparent truth in their scallop shapes

and our spidery nerves will vibrate,
then engage sight at the exact instant
the fluxing world arranges itself
in equal scallops, in patterns of the beast's proof
and that's the picture we receive,
that's the pattern our friends design
their behavior around.

The soft luster of Devine's leather coat
outshines sweet reason's light,
the ladder in Debra's mind aligns her pals in rungs,
Sugar flashes on lines of cocaine, a gunbarrel
and bright facets of bullet-splintered glass
fill George's eye entirely.

A person hooked on the beast's glittering wares
becomes unthinking huckster,
one tooth on a lit saw
extending human to human to his hustler lip,
clothesrack to his threads, showster
for his autos, doorperson to his patriarchy,
mind for his thoughts and face
a cameo of his scintillating glamour.

Smiling or surly glamour
we're able to defuse, to depower

by moving back and gently laughing,
"That one's sucked into the beast's maw,
swallowed his bait hook, line and sinker."

And acquaintances can follow his charms,
ride the great coruscating tide
or pull back behind secure walls
and exorcise, cut friends out
of their lives for self-survival:

shutting doors on junk the ex-junkie
shuts doors on all his old buddies,
Stevie's lover withdraws and counts his change
while her high-class voice out-vibes her body's wish
and she promenades the Sheraton alone,
Omega flakes out on a yacht, Bjorg on
climbing mountains, Jay scrambles into the rat race
and they've no time for Terry, Cathy or Chuck.

And we may confront our friends
if there's deep good feeling
to support a prideful conflict:

we pull at illusion tapes
their minds replay like recorders
and cling to as original thoughts,
use our clear-cut anger and most cutting ideas
to demolish the brain warps induced by beast logic
and still keep relaxed good will
in force at every sentence end,

our faces beaming human support
for a whole shaky being underneath

even as we rattle through changes the entire night,
all next day and the following week.

One outstretched arm embraces our friends
and the other prods at ignorant flaws
like two horns of the dilemma that
defines what we can decently do:

if we aren't gentle with friends
the larger gentle world is not possible,
and if friends aren't criticized
they won't change to help that world arrive.

Love is our guide. Even love unrecognized.

Unlustful, human love the force
that informs what changes can break down
beast-taught habits and resist the slanted shapes
our heads and bodies could assume.

In the hospital's marble john the ex-cop
risks naming my old pals in the beast's game:
"They're your worst fucking enemies," he says,
Seth insists the first and last battle
is the war for people's minds,
Louise sees classism everywhere, Jerry sexism
and they shout down workmates, hesitate

when feedback relates they'll soon create enemies.

Love's healthy drive is to receive information
and Boyes is its first proud spy,
"I love you," says Jack in the
foothill twilight that shines with true colors,
"I want you to live strongly."

Ron's mate asks reversal of 7 years' housecleaning
and he hears, picks up a mop as a new habit,
Nellie's love informs her how to ask
her partner to do his unmacho half
and he responds in bringing up their child.

Marge watches Bob's bloodshot eyes
as he lays the law down with tight-lip restraint
and she receives anger as anger,
my sisters and brothers say what's real
to their parents, mother and father
look through sixty-plus years and regard in earnest,
Huncke sat up all night with N.
who was sorting as best one can.

Carol learns to give herself
a little more respect than she gives others,
Ray figures if his energy is misused once
it's an accident, twice a coincidence,
three times: enemy action.
Barry did one thing each day to feel bad
until he joined the Psych Collective

in the months- and years-long struggle
to reclaim self-identity from the beast,
Grant's friends did nothing and he felt
nothing til a truck ran him down.

The beast trains us to feel bad
about ourselves and his soothing voice
presents old roles and ways to be
as the only ways we'll feel good

but we have a better choice,
to move toward each other with minds
to think and wills to coax
our own voice out from inside,

the inner voice that has respect for life
respects and loves the human babe
that rises through the debris of my own psyche
and of my friends' psyches. "I love you.
I want you to live strongly."

The struggle is unending.

Faces shine with hope and close in despair,
when I stare with hope in mind
the air may resonate and fan hope
alive again in other eyes and a new,
small flame can warm the human tide.

The struggle is unending.

Light blinks on and off
like the beacon of a pulsing star,
and the search itself for human light
unshutters light.

Love is our guide.

Six

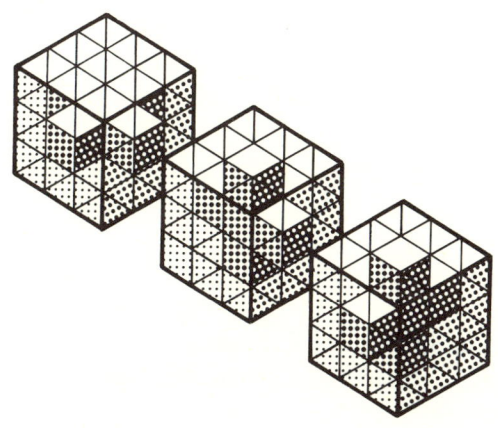

Not sure if we're not just lulled
into quiet rooms and given space
to play in as crucial muscles flab,
and as trains of thought relax

we become easy prey to the beast:

when will it suit him,
how much time is given us
before his fist crunches through the wall?

Or with a long-not-thought-over-thought
we finally become his suckered tools?

How long can we consult in storefronts,
develop muscles and practice moves
before through a forgotten back door like a
neighborhood dog, with wagging tail and watery eyes
sneaks the one debilitating blind spot?

How long can we exercise,
how long hesitate
before confronting the beast
on his own level of physical and mental violence?

How long will it hold, or will it bend,
the old rule that the means determines the end?

Will it shake to horrible uncertainty
as tracers split the sky into shards
and shudder into puffs, as walls
vibrate, bow in and tree-lined streets
take on contours of a continuous scream?

R. A. Olson, Fontana, Vicenzo, Stannek
are taken away and the cries
that never reached their lips
echo through my subconscious and wave
into an unending future like wind rippling
over a field of wheat, around me now
the lines of resignation sink deeper
as slow prints of a final boot.

Aunt Lois gave forty years to the factory

and twenty mothering her nephews concurrently,
with ample power to upend the train, send punks
to vegetable farms and managers to factories
we ride subways with eyes fractured in jigsaw pieces,
Wanda progresses from waitressing to dancing topless
to posing on a street corner,
Arturo counts his Chicano options on the
fingers of one hand: all poor.

It feels good to get angry.

To yell at this fucking place,
to scream anger into coherence,
to hitch fragments from our glossed-over past
with pain from economic traps,
with anger at my lopsided training,
to clean my guts' sourness with a long howl
that starts up from the soles of my feet,

it feels good to get angry.

In my dreams I'm not alone,
with many others I psych up higher
and higher and release a roar
that shakes the land.

Means are here.

Cramer's Valley scoops in, feeds, protects
those on the run and is known by another name,

R. leads relief over state lines
on a back route to Wounded Knee,
P. hands out larger and larger welfare checks
with flimsier and flimsier pretence.

In 1857, 1925, 1952 and throughout history
prisoners held their guards as last ditch
ransom for a very few rights
and sometimes began a reasonable dialogue,
Jackson stood up and lost his life
and did not die with unspoken pain on his lips,
black gunmen ambushed the first-sight enemy
in suicide pacts in Cleveland and in Oakland,
D. keeps up on bomb and gun technology.

In Arizona, in Sacramento, who knew how to
ignite munition trains and not hurt anyone!
G. blew up power lines in suburban hills,
S. the remaining pipeline between Bay oil refineries,
C. cracked over billboards with a bulldozer
to protest invasion of the most private property:
a human's nervous system.

L., G., A., K. and several decades' stream of bodies
lay down on railway tracks to Army depots,
swarmed a flotilla in front of carriers
in token blocking of the beast's passage
and transmitted in fact insistent nonviolence,
the Vietnamese know how many times successful!
Michael distributes firecrackers against Trident,

Nadja against a reactor,
N. J., Baraka stick to their guns.

This no accurate chronicle
but a smattering from the unheralded tide
the beast would swallow or ignore.
How can I tell of protest through the 19th century,
Knights of Labor, unions, the CP,
black freedom struggles, hobo trains in the thirties,
the Wobblies, the SWP, draft riots in New York,
women, old people, gays, the handicapped,
your grandparents', neighbors', siblings' actions?

How can I prove a case,
what can I do but point to a network of pain
and call it political?

Means are here. We use them

in the basic war for minds, to open
the flow of free and accurate information.

In People For Science, Science For People
Metsler fumes on ecology and energy:
"Traditional companies continue traditional methods
for traditional profits even though
we have valid solutions today,"
Africans point to a continent where
foreign clouds flash red from civil gunfire
the beast ignites abroad, in the fight for ERA

the politicians' repeated show of conscience
Keith labels: "shadowplay,"
Anita prescribes against a macho union:
candy in one hand, a gun in the other
and adroitness in using both.

Indians march. The Dutchman on teargas:
wet sand sewn in a canvas pad with two straps,
one tied to the wrist, one held in the same hand
and released as a captured cannister is slung back.

Means are here. We use them

through months under red-inflamed skies
and squeezed out of shape, or while nature
parades serene days and puffball clouds
soberly we develop a soldier's style of life
in small, tough ways that we can.

Joan responds with equal force to her would-be raper,
Karen meets male eyes on the street, holds their gaze
and transmits, "I'm not looking at a lay,"
Lucy spews anger at every slight gesture
a male makes hinting dominance,
S. rages at his training to be the patriarchy's goon,
slams his every second thought
and forms a men's group, shaking and game,
tired having his gonads tugged
Larry scrawls on a billboard promoting 50 static feet
of beautiful flesh: "Necrophilia!"

We display the puzzling of beast moves,
set our struggle into unavoidable black and white,
blaze his skeleton with brightest anger
on plain walls for all eyes to see
the same as gamma rays burned on Hiroshima's walls
the shape of *homo sapiens.*

On a transit tunnel in fluorescent paint
the obvious avoided message:
"Attica equals My Lai, Saigon equals New York,"
across town on a roadside building
"Socialism is only fair," "Vote, stupid!"
and what equals the sign "Coca-Cola"
at 35 hundred meters on Inca stonework?
The bank's billboard "Where do they get the money?"
has its stencilled answer:
"From the workers, of course."

Words from our minds,
pointed fingers, bodies and lives
pose as question marks and careful splats of anger

all signposts we read and will remember,
will score as depth soundings of a groundswell
and take with future sights
as bases for action and information to aid
in bringing the hidden currents
to surface tides.

Means are here.

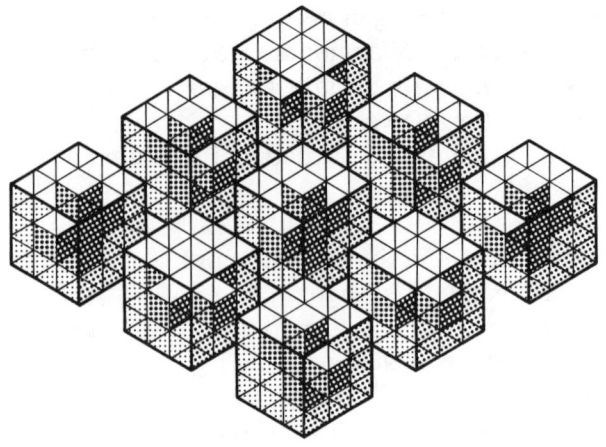

Seven

The fight begun has its own dilemma:

beginning battle begins corruption of life's beauty
that did convince me absolutely
it's worth fighting for,
in prehistory's first encounter the first club-swing
stunned beauty, and it's been vibrating
through warped shapes ever since.

Those who've begun
gain deep relief of action
and yet remove easy peace from their lives

as houses pull aslant with tension,
faces go awry and the most level looks
still guarded as minds envision the law
knocking on the door, with guns still holstered
and subpoenas not yet delivered:

pretend we're so divided
we don't know our best friends.

The fight begun has its own traps,

what's done in deep-felt indignation
has its social content ignored
and the most heartless effects
splattered across newspapers:
"WATTS 40 BLOCKS IN FLAMES"
"PRISON RIOT LEAVES 5 DEAD"
"TERRORIST BOMB HITS CITY BANK"
black-ink spice in the culture's food
heats more uninformed passions,

hysteria an easy tool in the beast's horny hands.

Human nature easy prey to his ploy:

be a revolutionary like Roy, like A. with tough manners,
rough unbullshitable speech furry with glamour,
shoulders flex and tirades echo
when trucks gather in the rear forty,
cycles pull up at coffeehouses

and nothing's done. Nothing committed.

Or what's done for change is so extreme:

once courage is screwed to zinging heights
our heads distort, sight bends
and we continue for sake of pride
into arenas where we're not competent:
the Village bomb factory explodes,
the SLA house burns in a blaze of gunfire
and we flame the sky with our mistakes

as viewers turn away in horror.
Cell-shocked horror never to forget
the vengeful flame of modern armories.

Still the battle repeats the same old story,

the Dutchman goes to the riot's front line
to look the enemy in the face
and sees a blond, blue-eyed country boy
and his third-world brother
following orders and drawing pay:

nothing new. Nothing new either

when Lisa follows an ideal to her energy's end,
spews truth from podiums through a mouth
so taut and stance so haggard
her body transmits: sickness.

And a thought acted cleanly
or an act cleanly related
conveys beyond itself the relationship between people
it contains at its beginning:

the Front's synchronized attacks
are made by comrades taking orders from a male,
Bar's mouth rolls out hard gems that ring true
and are polished with lips of purest blueblood,
the wing of Command's impassioned reason
is feathered with burr-edge hate,
Ned talks his prick into a viable dyad,
Jones squeezes the unfair world into a scheme
and both dictate the procedures:

a word from on high is received by sheep.

Even on basic levels the dilemmas:

once our lives are meshed with revised attitudes
then comes the struggle to survive
the world's onslaught as different people,
next comes the tooth-on-edge struggle
to keep our thoughts clear as they're set
on human tongues and breathed into air.

Marx on economics, Firestone on sex roles,
Weil on self-esteem, Mao's words
on work for need not profit
distort in convoluted ear whorls

and faces spin around or partly away
like leaves in a shifting breeze.

Political problems compound as life adds its dilemmas:

one force will become its opposite,
a vigorous plant shoot tightens bark
around its base in time,
a young ape about-faces and fights off
siblings after its rush to power.

Archie invests so much in a leftist stance
later to protect the money he becomes right-wing,
with eyes blazing Liz fights sexism so hard
she loses touch with her feelings,
C. and B.'s momentum to get a collective rolling
pulls them around in boss's roles.

Reaching into the ideal
how often does an open hand
turn as if into water and bend back
showing tangled hair and claws?

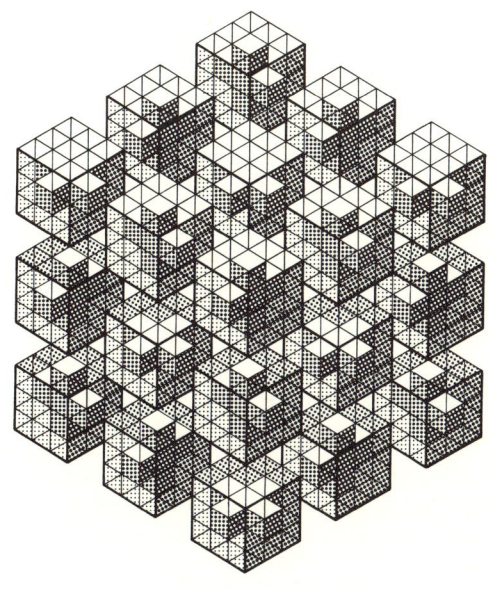

Eight

Who dares confront dilemmas
in political thought and action,
who dares look beyond contradictions
that loop forward motion into circles
or put hostile lenses on clear eyes

that one dares peel complex masks

off a plain face and simple acts,

dares not to avoid the obvious.

Obvious: we are exploited.

Sal, Joe and the laborers work for others' profit
in barter for a little wealth, tough-it-out attitudes
and most of their lives sweating,
developing sciatica, cancer, or piles

and under an orange hard-hat the beast is smiling.

Suburban siblings do the beast's professional work
and harden their arteries, their lives and families
trapped in a cycle of cars, houses, pools,
future bank payments and uncertain credit,

in a pin-striped suit the beast is smirking.

Marie poses by a mantle, Jody by the balustrade
and the rich classes retain pleasures, de-fuse minds
and have their style spread through magazines, TV
as models for us to imitate or aspire to,

above a low-cut dress the beast is sneering.

Sweethearts agree to perform well in jobs
and arrange efficient roles under pressure
of coming mouths to feed, exchange rings,

kiss at the altar and opt out of risky action,

above a black collar the beast smiles paternally.

Mary Lou, Gordon and the students are given
time to work, grow and achieve good grades
as along as they succeed in rising higher
through the middle classes and prove upward mobility,

in cap and gown the beast is gloating.

D. scuffles through a cycle of drugs, theft, jail,
Laura ambles through dress, lovers, patois
and how many coteries give up wholeness
in payment for the praise "hip" or "with it,"

behind mirrored shades the beast's eyes are laughing.

On street corners gangs eye each other,
"spiks" "niggers" "crackers" "slopes" "hippies"
flare energy in rumbles and lower-class foes
keep each other down by reason of race,

the beast leans on a siren and cheers.

Past shanty huts, past the corner store,
stubbing toes in a gully Georgia belts out,
"Pick your raisins off the shitpie!
If you've ever tried to live,
if you'll ever have to die

the system sucks from either end.
Pick your raisins off the shitpie!
If you've ever had to rent,
if you've ever tried to buy
the system sucks from either end.
Pick your raisins off the shitpie!"

Streets ripple with frustration, hookers and the trade
invite abuse of human bodies for a price,
brass-knuckle and gunned-up groups
look for something to rip off,
so many feeling ripped-off inside

and as he sucks the beast is smiling.

Obvious: the system's geared to profit.

And beast tapes run through our minds,
direct us to make bucks,
trick us to run in places useful to others' profit
or repeat a thousand excuses why
we should do nothing for change.

We pass his words parent to offspring, we spin on words
sibling to sibling, friend to friend
and the beast smiles as we do his work.

Victims of victims of victims *ad infinitum,*
victims of victims live by the beast's information,
we too are victims who would change him.

Do you know what your mouth is saying,
have you heard what your ear is listening to?

Would you reject this information because of its style
or quarrel with its soft line
when real change requires movement through all sectors,
not come from any particular quarter but a
tide everywhere generous, accepting, forward-moving,
through all my mind and body as through the country,
from North, East, South, West, from across
the mountains, swelling up in the midlands?

Before the gilded storefront, in coffee-stained rooms
Ann snaps at those on the same broad road,
"That's no way to start a movement!"
and the beast tugs up her friends' fists:
don't you see he's pleased with divisiveness

as he mouths their words, "Right on!"?

The half-decent politician promises
a new siphoning-off toward less unequal riches
while the rip-off assumes new forms, no accident
that Cabinet members resemble pigs, and after Watergate
the beast waves a laundered flag: do you believe

his upright posture and clean-shaven face?

In the courtroom under pressure to fight or change
a collective macho ego opts out of humanity

in using language without truth as a tool:
can you feel delight when the beast preens

in judge's robes and bangs his gavel, "Case closed!"?

Consciously the town council invites in big business,
apartment complexes and taxes small people
out of their homes, their unconscious
kill- and rape-derived thrills spur on
the group scheme to make money: can you imagine

the beast fingers tickling their animal nerves?

So many men work so hard to realize
their father's dreams and out-perform their brothers
they don't know what they want
or what they feel, and the beast
has got them by the balls: do you hear his guffaw

as he squeezes a little harder?

While most sisters remain weirdly paid servants
to husband and home, Tina becomes adroit
at a lathe, Joan behind a truck wheel
and the media imply women are now liberated:
do you hear the beast titter

as he puts on a wig, bumps and speaks soprano?

Jimmy picks failure, Jamie picks lovers

who deal pain, punkers pick alienation from the air
with knives, safety pins, staples and stick it
in their bodies, at last they identify
what fingers strike: but do you see their limbs

are just gloves for the beast's fingers?

Marie gets involved in co-workers' lives, their dress,
their children's careers, Bert in work's details,
in talk by the coffee-machine, in deals
on the side and both stand the tedium:
do you hear bored laughter as the beast

siphons their energy and whispers, "That's life!"?

Moocksar measures heavy metals in heart muscles:
too much radiation already and his boss demands,
"Present your result in a most favorable light:
we (the industry) need (profit from) nuclear energy,"
can you see the beast's hypocrite smile

as true data is reported on a slant?

Dan tries to confront the beast
and finds he keeps hiding, no keypunch board,
no vote booth, no committee really responds,
follow one aisle into a polite office and its doors
revolve with smiles, referrals, forms:

if the beast can he'll stay hidden.

Vickie sees him in a vision, walks the tile floors
and green halls where the beast lives,
feeds computer cards to a tenacle on a desk
that sticks up like an alien toe of chrome and plastic
and the walls vibrate with husky energy,

can you hear the beast humming his tune?

Why he runs is no mystery.

Victims of victims of victims *ad infinitum*,
victims with a higher class and dollar signs
in their eyes direct all energy
to move up rungs on his long ladder
that leads up from the ground and then turns
its direction to sideways while a grinning beast

pumps his organ, "Merrily We Go Around."

Oh let him smirk.

There's no last laugh for him.

On the inside of this country we're imprisoned
by a few poor agreements between many humans,
on the inside of my head the voices I hear
to the right, to the left, across the roof of my skull
form corridor walls that guide my behavior
and the light ahead is just a glimmer
from the prison courtyard.

Let the beast grin.

There's no last laugh for him.

With the truth told
the walls around are known for prison bricks,
the halls of our minds are heard to resound
with clever tricks of internal guards.

With the truth told
embroidered costumes are stripped
from the beast's gross hide,
once seen no natty dress, no dimmed or flashing lights
can blind eyes to his protruding bones,

obvious: the system's geared to profit.

And what's obvious can be fought.

There are decades to go,
future minds will open for flow
and clear knowledge is at hand today,
at hand also is the barely-tapped energy
of a tide of humans who would
open portals to a greener world.

The obvious is handle on the door to change.

There's no last laugh for the beast.

Nine

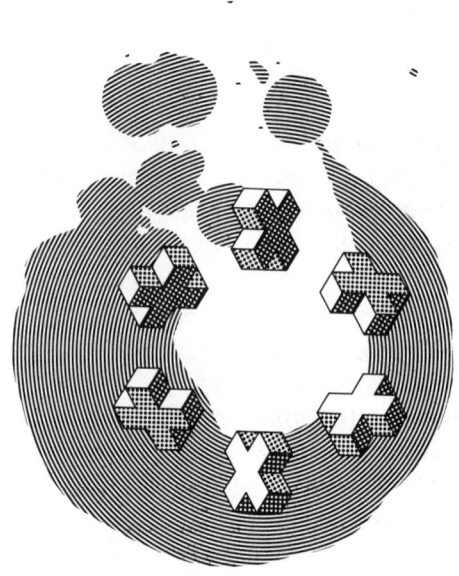

Not ours either: there's no last laugh

but one task follows another task in a
linked chain from the distant past into the future,
insight leads to decision leads to trial
of old and new levers we use to pry down
walls in our minds and to jam, tamp
or ease open the door to change.

The nature of the beast is ours to rearrange.

Each thought and each act for change
does change our lives,
and every changed life is change in the beast
whose flesh, bone, innards and brain
is composed of humans,
whose every cell is a human being.

We are parent to the beast.

Each act between people
forms a geometric unit that can be repeated
into the total structure of the system,
each act continues the system's bent for profit
or turns it toward serving our lives.

Every act is political.

Chris paints an "X" on Welfare Department doors,
her rating for how people are screwed there,
in vote booths a multitude tries to X-out taxes
that do not serve us, R. takes off the hundred pounds
he buried feeling under and stands his ground,
a Situationalist rollers the businessman's sign down

to one message: "You count."

Helene stands on City Hall steps
with her retarded child in arms and demands rights,

Roxie carries her mother through the streets,
"If you see how they treat old people here
you'll pray to God, take you early,"
Hannah's head pounds when her hospital bill arrives:

"I know what I'm sick from: capitalism."

The beast's doctor interrupts a birth,
turns the kid upside down, cuts its cord,
shocks it with a slap and says, "You're mine,"
and the gray in Lisa's eye turns to steel
when her daughter comes home crying,

"Now the war's on for my child's mind!"

Sandy, Phil organize a union,
Karen, Maggie, Heidi, Selina, Valerie
grip tools largely denied to women,
Brookhall opens doors to his shop,
Lurke takes on apprentices,
George takes a partner in an honest business,
Stu teaches self-defense, Laura learns it,

Stevie takes matters in her own hands.

Women talk to each other about what's real,
begin pushing back the 4,000-year-old invasion
of their minds and bodies by men,
Carol uses her rare position to hire women,
Dan hears "Women's liberation is liberation for men"

and watches a mirror for his jawline's curve,
Morgan cringes at her sister's lacy dress:

"Wake up to how you're using yourself!"

Nadja was high on skiing, Manfred on ballcourts,
Randy on sex, Jay on bucks, Dennie in psych sessions
and they close their lids, watch the screen split
into swirling orange and green of the beast's iris,
Michael opens his eyes in a dark night, sees the glow
of plutonium dust on clapboard walls

and tells himself, "Do something. Anything."

We're vulnerable to con if we avoid real feelings,
workaday's eight hours and then TV a drug,
soap operas and valium aid suburbia's tranquility,
drugtown's ritual: "Give me librium or give me meth,"
prisons' carbon monoxide, asylums' thorazines,
universities' avoidance of sweet reason for today:
the disciplined statement of powerful feeling.
Jan exhults naivete, "Even one half step away from

heartfelt outrage begins the bullshit."

If I know who you are we have a chance
of making contact, says Jeanette,
"I have difficulty enough with life's realities
without shilly-shallying around the beast's bush,"
Felicia, Tom, Opal tell the truth,

the genius begins taking people seriously
and friends look him in the eye, speak first lines

of a decent contract: "Don't betray me."

The thief pays his taxes when his victims
replace their stereos, the drifter's hosts
pay his share of wages to Nebraskan soldiers
who stand ready to twist two brass keys
that would launch a wave of SIOP's nuclear missiles,
as a child I shielded my eyes
from the shit coming down the family line
and the beast keeps pushing my hand up
over half-closed lids, his most clever wile

is to convince us he doesn't exist.

But yes: the beast exists.
We are his parent.

If we forget the Rosenbergs and their defense
still their framed political murder
is a dark area in my subconscious
that directs me away from dangerous action,
George Jackson, the SLA, Weatherpeople are felt
as isolated incidents, Eric's attitudes are shoved
in an irrelevant box: "60's-type thinking,"
but as I sample leftist work there's far too much
going on for me to follow,
the beast's second cleverest wile

is to convince us WE don't exist.

But yes: we exist.
We are parent to the beast.

The light at the end of dugout tunnels
is very small and Jo-Jo leaves playground ball
for a chance to kick up sand in a larger field,
Terry starts the radical fifth wheel in a
conservative union, Judy becomes socialist feminist,
Dick joins anarchists, Mike learns from his own anger
and asks, "Once you know all this, what then?"

The simple answer: "Stay alive."

S., H., T. give spare energy to a socialist school,
working for small causes Mona trains for the
most broad cornerstone for change: community organizing,
Robbie W. in rape counselling, Robbie S. in wife abuse
bring awareness to the beast's slimy underside,
Ron works in classes to raise consciousness
and passes on the lead he maintains:

one half-jump ahead of the beast.

The block figures how to vote correctly,
George worries whether to make bombs,
Z. lends a hand, accepts that terrorists
are a legitimate part of the community,
Darrel climbs professionally,

buys a house and declares it safe,
in David's, Don's, Karen's, Lisa's guts the problem:
how to earn what they need and yet live ideals,
James insists: pick health for your own being,

in every life there's room for effective action.

In the bank's line I overhear the greenback blues,
"Work hard all day and still be broke,"
when I have money I have dignity
and the rich here have so much more than the poor
(2 plus some multiplied by 10 to the 5th power)
and the gap is widening.
Why not narrow the ratio
to three (for families) to one (for singles)?
My brand-new store-bought feelings
last just so long as the shine on my new shoes
and the market wall is split with a red line,

"Are you busy being born, or are you busy buying?"

Paul works for a general strike believing
any small strike is against us in the long run,
but those with asbestosis, black lung
or working in sun-baked fields with bags
over their heads have a different view,
aware of the little by little we can actually do
Sam insists, "Short run, long run, bah!

What counts is the left turn."

George learns care from his union's mistakes
and any front's errors are lessons to mind,
my next move will be unique to suit
the next situation coming down the pike.
They aid the struggle also who turn their backs
and say their clear human reasons,
scrawled on a slab wall under live oaks
is the Dragon's cue, "Let those who will do nothing

for the revolution, do nothing against it."

We are parent to the beast.

A multitude of people create the beast
in agreeing to give human greed
wide play,
yet any humans who look each other in the eye
and say
an unhostile word that can be understood
also agree on respect
as the bottom line, also agree to accept
the other as a being like oneself,
also agree to siblinghood.

Those who agree the game is to exploit each other
already agree on cooperation
and the telling difference is:
which we make the law.

Which agreement is basis for our behavior.

We are parent to the beast.

He is ours to train, to change, or to eliminate.

As beings in control of our selves
we have the power
to take the beast out of the jungle,
though he will return
with con, smiles and perennial scowls
in every new system, in every new arena

he's here only for a while: kiss him good-bye.

We are creators of his life
and instruments of his demise.

Glorious the business day
when he spreads his wares on a multi-color mat
and there are no takers: put him on welfare.

Or let him fight to the end,
on a red Sunday we'll open his guts to the sky
from end to end, split him crotch to skull
and let his juice flow into the earth.

Build him a tombstone for all eyes:

"Here lies the beast
that pulled old tricks out of new bags for centuries,
master of oppression and fakery,

        overcome by a multitude of humans
        who hereby assert our dignity.
        Rest in Peace,
beast that allowed us neither while he reigned."

We are instruments of his demise
and the owners of our lives,

when his paw is taken from my back
my unbounded heart will ring like a bell
with its cracks and fissures healed at last,

when his claw is taken from my mind
I will be free, I can put the energy released
from the battle into creation at last,

when our wishes are no longer clouded
by the beast's scowl, our common desire
will have a chance to dream its details into clarity,

when our days are removed from his law
our common desire for a pleasant life may spread
across the land in a clear-rayed dawn.

Clive Matson was born in Los Angeles in 1941 and grew up on an avocado ranch in northern San Diego County. He served an apprenticeship to poetry in New York City in the 1960's and has worked at a variety of jobs. He has been active in the East Bay Men's Center, the Bay Area Socialist School and at present he counsels men who batter. He lives in Oakland and leads the Garnet poetry workshop. His previous books are EQUAL IN DESIRE (1982), HEROIN (1972), SPACE AGE (1969) and MAINLINE TO THE HEART (1966). He enjoys playing basketball and collecting minerals in the field.